NU Moon

Poems, Short stories, and quotes on Healing and Growth

ISBN: 978-1-387-49659-4

Written by Yulli Bouza

Design by Yulli Bouza.

For Him. For Her. Forever Love. God is Love.

About the Author

Who is Yulli Bouza aka "QueenPoetLove"? Yulli Bouza is an Afro-Cuban, American writer, poet, psychotherapist, and creative speaker who believes deeply in the power of healing and transformation through truth and spoken word. She uses her creativity to manifest light and healing in the lives of others through her poetry, writing, and speaking. Her writing and poetry express her life experiences, growth, evolution, and truth, so that others may be freed from their wounds. Yulli writes to empower and to demonstrate the power of love with her passion for creativity. Yulli Bouza is a host to her podcast "Not Your Average Queen'' and "Divine Alignment", where she promotes self-help and a positive mindset. A mother to two beautiful daughters and married to her purpose mate Joel Renaud, Yulli incorporates all of her life experiences to help others on their path to finding the truest versions of themselves.

"I pray my love serves you well"---Yulli B

Journey

No one ever talks about the journey it takes to reach healing.
The recalling of pain.
The memories that haunt our thoughts like ghost.
The arguing with ourselves to accept our reality OR convincing those that hurt us that we hurt
We never see the struggle of overcoming generations of trauma.
Just to come out unprovoked, untriggered, and unbothered by what our wounds used to feel like.
Trying daily to get it right
I pray that your healing brings you unwavering power.
Strength on the days that your abuse makes you feel like a coward.
As if molestation was not hard enough to devour.
Like being raped in trusting someone you honor.
The deepest brokenness comes from those we give all the power
There is a journey to healing wounds of an unapproving mother
Or an unavailable father
Using sexuality to become empowered
Running to idols to feel like we matter
silenced by secrets that grow like towers
becoming monuments of excuses that multiply by the hour
We promise ourselves that we will do better
Better in expressing our pain and not allowing our anger to make us bitter.
Bitterness is the seed of hate that grows,
In dirt
In darkness
In soil that seems unworthy
But in the end finding that beauty shines above unkept ground
and real transformation starts underneath everything that we keep in, safe and sound
And this is the journey that we embark on, once release the shame of our scars that bound

Find ME

Sometimes we want someone to pour into us
Like we pour into them
We crave being filled in areas,   q we never knew existed
And have resisted for so long with hopes
for someone else to find
Find ME

Everything isn't Reciprocated

Losing a hand
To gain a hand
When you take, you give
When you give,
You take.
Everything isn't reciprocated

Not Sorry

to those who you may offend
let your change be absolutely necessary
because
When you are growing, you no longer have anything to defend

Flow Through Me

Deep
Is the river that flows through Him
Who flows through me
In the summer,
the water rushes upon me,
warm,
Kissing every part of my soul
Deep is the river that flows through Him
Who flows through me

Healing

Healing hast to be the mending of pain with rebirth
The connection between beautiful
and torn.
The transformation of brokenness into growth

Girls will be girls

(A Short Story)

There is a girl that needed to be loved, because in whatever lifetime she existed previously she did not feel valued or appreciated. She was never recognized by her peers or family. Her talents and gifts never fulfilled. She spent her life depressed with the desire to feel important. She used hardness to mask her pain. She drank endlessly. This girl also wandering with the romance of becoming everything she knew she could be. But she lived constantly in fear. She feared the unknown. She feared failure because she did not know what it felt like to win. She used her sensuality to get what she wanted. Attention, money, gifts. Girls will be girls.

Painless Death

Sometimes we need a cure
To ease hurt and wash regret with strength
Death is not always physical
We die daily without knowledge or direction
Death is mental
Sometimes painless because we lack correction

"Little things say a lot about you."—Yulli B

Waste of love

There are people who waste
love
They either don't know how to love you
or don't know what to do with your love.
Just wasting love

What is worth

What is it worth
If you never find peace
If you take more than you give
If you give more than you have to give
If it's too much to ask
If asking is too much
if You are stuck and your life hasn't begun
What is it worth
If you never live

People, please

I can no longer show up for people like I used
Peace is my new priority
I have healed from pleasing people

Identity crisis

It is like a puzzle
To a maze
That we can't see
A labyrinth of toxic and spirituality
Searching and drowning in ancestral debt
In need of a true reality
Finding yourself
In an ocean of cries
Tainted by every lie
That has traumatized me
Trauma abused the hell out of the seed
And how can we grow
To know
To show
That there is peace in freedom
There is a crisis
In accepting truths
In loving you
In honoring you
In trusting you
In being you
In being true
In discovering you
In you

My poetic gift

I'm in my poetic gift today
Because poetry was a gift to me
By all things Divine
You see poetry saved me
In my demise
In my wine
In my time
Poetry gave hope
Poetry gave vision
Poetry gave me purpose
I am in my poetic gift today
Because poetry was a gift to me
By the Divine
To discover the Divine
In my crying
In weeping
In my seeking
Poetry gave me power
I am in my poetic gift today
Because poetry was a gift to me,
So Divine
In my destruction
In my growth
Poetry birthed
A Queen in this ethereal world
I am in my poetic gift today
Because poetry was a gift to me, so right

Don't

Don't let me stay
Don't let me stay
Don't let me stay
Where I am not wanted
Where I am not needed
Where I am not seeded
Don't let me stay
Where I am not growing
Where I am not flourishing
Where I am not transforming
Don't let me stay
Where I am not loved
Where I am not love
Where I am not one with God
Don't
Don't let me stay
Where I am not valued
Where I have no value
Where I am undervalued
Don't
Let
Me
stay
Where I am not accepted
Where I am arrested
Where I am neglected
Where I am rejected

Don't

Don't let me stay
Where I am broken
Where I am mourning
When I am weeping
When I am seeking
Don't let me stay
Where I am miscarrying
When I am aborting
Where I am hurting
Don't
Don't let me stay
Where I am abused
Where I am misused
When I am of no use
Don't let me stay
When I am raped
When I am molested
Don't let me stay
Don't let me stay
Don't let me stay
Where I am
Don't let me stay
Where I am famished
When I am hungry
When I am thirsty
When I am searching
Don't let me stay
Where I am lonely
Where I am depressed
Where I am dead
Don't let me stay

Where I am begging
Where I am yearning
Where I am not learning
Don't
Done let me stay
Don't let me stay
Don't let me stay
Where I am not walking in my
Divine Supreme Power

Being A Mother

I am afraid
To birth so close to death
That I would bleed to the pit

Torn.

Torn
To pieces
With no peace of
Him
Of
You
Of every season that burns of you
Torn
With feelings
Of wanting more
In needing more
Of him
In you
Torn

Needing

When I am needing
It's not always a soft touch
But a soft voice to soothe
My inner pains
The hurts no one sees
Because I am too busy being mommy,
Bae or the dish washing maid
Needing
Is the need to be embraced
Not on days when you remember
But because your existence
Was made to love me
Hold me
Needing
Care
Value
And appreciation
Because my needs are just as important
Then chores
Loving me is not a task you forget
Needing
To be showered
In the sweetest gesture of
Your giving
Because adornment is the smile
Of a well-loved woman
Needing

Effort

Effort is the action of thought

The initiation of gesture and concern.

A simple demonstration of what we desire to obtain.

When you want something strongly, you put in maximum effort

Just giving

Sometimes we get comfortable in how people love us
That we don't expect more than the bare minimum.
Actually, just the minimal.
No thoughts,
Just whatever is giving

Meet at equilibrium

Match my scared because I am holy
Like white on Sunday
 I am Risen Divine consciousness
Never forsaken
If you are looking for me,
Meet at equilibrium

Raw

The reality is that life isn't always perfect
Sometimes we choose the wrong people
We make poor decisions
We fail to love ourselves
We envy others
We hate God
We lack self esteem
Sometimes we do our jobs better than we chase our dreams
Sometimes depression consumes us and
Anxiety is a daily struggle
Trusting others is easier than trusting ourselves
And we never get things right

Don't muzzle me

What I'm saying is that I poured my all into you and
 it destroyed me
Don't muzzle me

"A Person can know everything and still get everything wrong."- Yulli B

She was insecure

She killed everyone else
Running from herself
If you know her, you knew
That she existed but never overcoming her own demons,

Behind

What is not walking with me,
Beside me,
Or within me
I am leaving it behind

Connection

There are just some people we connect to.
Magnetic.
Easy.
Attraction,
That makes every moment fun
We have those people that we just vibe with,
Laugh the entire time.
No bad intentions
No jealousy
Just pure love
I want these connections

Revolution

This is my revolution
I am blazing all the guns
I'm starting a war
And in the end
I want to know I came in raging
And my wounds will become
Memories of my victory

Effort #2

If I must initiate everything,
I don't want your efforts

Untitled (short passage)

You are not supposed to lose yourself in love. I think at some point in life, we lose ourselves in love. If not in our romantic relationships, friendships, or family roles. We find ourselves over-playing our roles for validation or self-gratification. Whatever the reason, neither is healthy. If you have to lose yourself in love, then your over-doing love. Step back!

SuperPower

when love kills me,
I rise again
like a Phoenix
and that's my superpower

True Love

Some people love themselves so much, they can't love anyone else.
Other people don't love themselves enough, they don't know how to love anyone else.
Then there are people who love others more than they love themselves.
Neither is true love.
I have neglected myself for the sake of loving someone else.

Father wound

I want to know what it feels like to be in love,
All in
Without fear
I want to give my all with love
And receive the same in return
I want honesty
I want transparency
I want vulnerability that breaks walls of wounds
I want love that cures
All my father wound

Tired

I'm tired of learning from pain....

Progress Not Perfection (short passage)

Let's normalize progress, the small growths when overcoming failure. Perfection always seems easy, but what is really hard is knowing that life will never be perfect no matter how many things we get right. In a world where we are always striving for "picture perfect", let's normalize not having it all together all the time.

Potential

Potential
Keeps you in a fantasy with what reality could be
An idea that seems promising
But no real evidence of what's true
Potential keeps expectations unreachable
A prepaid balance of what is due
Holding hostage, the hope of something beautiful
But with an obstructed view

Transformation

Transformation only comes when we are ready. We aren't forced to change but when we can no longer resist the push of circumstances, then we become stuck between two positions. Transformation or remaining the same. If we keep failing ourselves, we will never reach our full potential. Do not be afraid to change.

Affliction

Sometimes I feel like I am begging God
Pleading
And this is my affliction

Never

Never stop
But we never started
Still waiting
But waiting
Never counting
Staying
Never satisfied
critical
Needing and yearning to be filled
Broken + empty
Never leave your happiness
In the lap of fools
Never

Just speaking

Did I fail myself again
What is failure if not
A tool
To leverage pain
Into opportunities of growth
Did I fail you
Because I wasn't sure
That you needed me more
Then I wanted me
Did I walk away wanting
More
Because more is just
A repetition of less
But don't give me any less
Then I am giving you
Because this is not a test
A test of time
A school of Lies
How long can my heart be silent
If it still cries
 within
Did I say that again?

Divine Consciousness

To be conscious means,
To be aware
But we can never wake, if we are too woke
And we can't see, if Third Eye blinds ego,
becoming too deep in false positivity
for the sake of appearing DIVINE

Answers

Sometimes we wait for answers
To questions we already know the answer to
But fear that our answers are wrong
Or maybe we didn't ask the question right
Therefore, we may have missed the real
Answer

Healing + Love

To be healed is the metamorphosis of love
But to love you must transform,
Trauma into pain and feel.
Because you can't heal what you don't feel

Urge

I want you to have an urge to experience,
the most celestial peace
that ever existed

Beautiful

A redefining meaning of perception
With prose
You are now my muse
And it is sweet
And it is bitter
In this moment, although it kills me, everything is poetry and
It is beautiful

I wanted.

I wanted this
Incomparable feeling of belonging
A need of constant satisfaction
The desire of a million lifetimes fulfilled
The sweetness gratitude brings only
When your love is reciprocated
Until you catch all the feels
I wanted a shining knight
To armor the days, I needed safety
A place
Where I could be myself and be supported with peace
Peace is a luxury
That we all don't experience
Peace of mind
Peace of heart
Peace of spirit
I wanted something simple
Like a love that I didn't have to heal

Over your head

Sometimes you have to let things go
Go where they came from
Where you thought they needed to be
Let them find a place
That is most fitting
Even if it isn't where they should be
Because we think we should
Put them where we want them
But not where they are supposed to be
Don't let that go over your head

"You Can't Heal what you don't feel."---Yulli B

"Sometimes hate and anger drive motives that lead to change."--Yulli B

"A person will leave you believing that there is something better than what they gave you"- Yulli B

"Everyone is vindictive in some way or form, no one is righteous."_---Yulli B

"Don't start anything you don't want unfinished"—Yulli B

Don't kill her

When a woman is angry
She is deadly.
Her words create curses that
Burn worlds of love with rage

Everything is geometry

Love is the one thing
Designed to make us human
Insecurities are anchors in our soul
Everything is geometry
Shapes of dimensions we can't control
We study and learn nothing
Painted between space and time
Traveling eons in search to find
The one to enlighten our core
Distance between balance and creation
A point from where we are never freed
Divinity Rising
The eye an object to those who see
If only we awaken Divine
Sacred of the one to all knows
Everything is geometry
Shapes of dimensions we can't control
Love is the one thing designed to make us human
Wounds are portals of untraveled galactic source
Healing flows without time
God is space of activity that connects the points that reveal more

Release and Let Go

What I'm releasing isn't for anyone but myself
I'm letting go what I have allowed to trap me in fear
Fear of what taking risks can unfold
Fear of embracing the power I behold
Forgiving all those who have come and go
I no longer hold pain as way to abuse myself long after the hurt
As we travel life, we have a tendency to hold on to things
 but today I Release and Let go

"A relationship of peace has both harmony + love"—Yulli B

"You are not supposed to lose yourself in love"—Yulli B

Run

We are trying to escape a
Truth that we can't deny
Seeking power in entities that are higher than earth
To find that we can run from ourselves
But we can't hide from our hurt.

"Broken Man" (short story)

He was wounded by his over critical mother. Unavailable to him because she wasn't available to herself. Running from her reality with numbing emotions, religion, money, and false beliefs of herself. Unable to help her son make sense of his own inner world. He couldn't go to her for healing. He found himself lost. Lost with how he was supposed to love a woman. Lost with how a woman was supposed to love him. Confused on how he needed to love anyone. This is a story of broken boy who became a broken man.

"You can't teach the unteachable"—Yulli B

"Don't listen to people who make too much noise. They often don't have too much to say"—Yulli B

"The prize is not in success but in the experience."---Yulli B

Dissociation (short story)

As a child he was molested and for a long time he didn't know what that meant for him. Sometimes he still doesn't know if he was truly done healing. Violation in any form is a disruption in identity. Dissociated from the present and his past. However, freed to know that he no longer was bound to any moment unless it provided safety.

Healing still

There are those who are healing, still.
Finding themselves in a wrong place
Or a hurt place, still
seeking to connect themselves to the part that they lost
In a memory, still.
or running from who they don't want to be, still.
Whatever the story, keep living.
Still.

Waiting on Perfection

Sometimes people will never meet our expectations
Of them
Or the person we want them to be for us
Because they just aren't who we think we want
And wanting them to be,
Is like waiting for perfection

Rush

We Rush into love
Or relationships
Just to say we have something
But
No matter how hard we try, we can't
Force time
Time is the only thing that functions without
Push or pull or force
However, it controls everything
The moment, the distance, the speed.
If we only allowed time to take time, we wouldn't be searching for more,
Because we never have to rush whatever we are not looking for.

"Our own defeat becomes our distraction"---- Yulli B

Eternally yours

When you find the one

That's breathes fire into your soul

Let love burn, eternally.

Because love that brings you alive is

A love that is always yours.

Wrong place, wrong time

Your love could've served me

Back when I didn't know my worth.

When mediocre efforts sufficed

Presently, a love that doesn't fulfill me

Is just wrong place,

Wrong time.

Parting ways

I'm parting ways with habits,

Ideas,

And things

That don't bring me into full

Completion of the woman I desire to be,

Farewell.

I love him

I love the things I have learned

And the things I find I had to unlearn

Through love with him.

Growth

True growth comes with

Understanding that change

comes with action.

I stop looking for things,

When I found everything in myself.

The broken woman (short story)

She was looking for love in all the wrong places. Needing to be fulfilled in the ways she desired because she thought it will fill the void of not having the father that she desired. Wanting to feel safe and protected under a man's embrace without fear. Because fear was all she knew. Fear that she would be abused like her father abused her mother. Fear that she would spend years with a man that ignored her existence. Fear that she would not find a love that would treat her like she knew she should be treated. A love that wasn't one sided, a love that wasn't violent, or destructive to her wellbeing. She feared that maybe she wasn't worthy of true love, because she was broken. Broken by disappointment, lack of trust, and trauma. This is a story of a broken woman.

The Golden Child (short story)

A boy filled with anxiety and low self-esteem. Highly unsure of himself and consumed with self-doubt. Never smart enough or good enough to meet his own expectations. Expectations imposed by his family. At school he was popular, had all the girls fawning over him. The best athlete, but hated himself.

Depression

I had moments
Of deep sadness
Hurt
Pain
Anger
Aggression
Regret
Resentment
The hardest to get out of
Is depression.
But there is always help. Seek help.

The insecure mom (short story)

Inside she was lonely and hated anything she couldn't be. She was hard. Hard mind and hard heart. Bullet proof. She taught her children how to be hard and emotionless. Also, superficial and arrogant. She never realized that her children needed the real her. The soft mom. But all they got was the insecure mom.

The scapegoat (short story)

The child everyone blames for everything. The truth teller but whose truth? Whose truth when reality was tainted with chaos and bouts of dissociation. What truth when every form of abuse was denied. Whose story are we telling?

Replay

Often times I replay
The past
Not for confirmation
But comfort
Because sometimes things seem easier
When we are past them
And not currently living them
I replay romance
As if it were still
Here
I reflect on the sweetness that brings innocence into
Full remembrance
Of holding hope near
I replay you
Like a past fear
Because today I am not sure
If we our future is clear

Honestly

In full honesty
Pain is the precept of change
If it doesn't hurt you
It does not move you
And if we remain still
We wither
Like leaves shedding anything
To remain true

NU moon

We visit a cycle of new beginnings
Entering a phase of continual shadow work
I learned that change requires accountability
I have discovered unfamiliar places I needed healing
Waves of emotions and fear move high and low
To reveal a light
That shines only in the dark
Hours
Of rebirth.

Soothe

That toxic love is something
That cradles every inch of our trauma
In insecurity
Afraid that complete healing
Will vanish the very passion of love
Unaware that we are bond
By the attachment of mommy and daddy issues
That are buried in the business of life
Just enigmas in our subconscious
That we act out with the ones we most dread
Dread that they are getting closer and closer to recollections we replay a million
times in our head
Questioning
Scared that if uncovered by our flaws
That we remain unlovable
And this what makes us hard
Hard because we try not let anyone in
Where the inner child is desperate to be freed
And the wounds of our past are greater than the knowledge
we seek
masking arrogance with bruises that constantly leak
in part of ourselves that are dying to be soothed

For my Husband

To my husband
If you are reading this,
Which I am pretty sure you are.
I love how you support me.
I just want to thank you for every effort you have made
To love me.
Thank you for walking with me in this lifetime and those before and those to come
Thank you for doing life with me.
You are special.
You are the giant in my heart
I keep in remembrance gratitude for all the things we have overcome.
Together we have purpose
And the transparency we have developed through our imperfections is worthy
I pray that our children will see a love
That is genuine and pure
And always believe in love that cures.

Soft

I am learning to be soft
Because that's apart of healing
 Because sometimes being hard
Meant I had numb what I was feeling
Feelings of inadequacy or self-doubt
masking weakness in strength
that didn't make me strong
buying into the idea
 that if I could overcome everything
I would make everyone proud

Evolution

Evolution
Is the ability to enter a different
Part of ourselves
Trusting that growth destroys old
Versions of who we are that are no longer serve
The person we are becoming

11:11

We receive confirmation daily
On where we should be going
Or what we should be doing
Synchronicity Speaking
Is seeing everything become what you have been seeing

Heaven

We are trying to reach Heaven
Through text, missed calls,and blocked calls
But no response
No where to leave a message.
If we only knew all the answers
We would know how to reach
Heaven
And touch what we are longing for
Because we are still longing,
To know what it takes to enter the gates with a calloused heart
Of Heaven

There is a river called Jordan`

Just along the side of destruction
Runs a water that flows,
a stream of hope that we all to seek to drink
floating along the edge we seek,
not knowing that the fruits are produced
not in how we live but in how we think

The Lost Tribe of Judah

Lost by those who love you
Overcome with your desires
to be free
A tribe amongst men of unfulfilled decrees

Undone

It took me a long time to get here
On the other side of who I was trying to overcome
Sometimes our own defeat consumes us
Because every time we thought we were whole, destruction was undone

Free

No longer tied, bound, or hostage
Be Free
From what keeps you tied
Be Free
From what keeps you bound
Be free
From what keeps you hostage

Grace

I feel like I am running out of time
I could have given up a long time ago
I can't even hear anymore
This must be a fall from grace

We war

We only war with ourselves
At least what is left of what we know
 Because suffering determines something
Maybe it will come back to me.
We always need someone
But we never hear what they see

Church hurt

It's hard to believe in the church
When those who are supposed to pray about you
Are the very ones that open wounds of hurt

Survival Mode

If I had to tell you what suffering looked like
I would say it was lonely
Silent on the days I needed to be heard
Crying when I had no words
An automatic response to feeling empty yet filled with so much to hold
Exploding consumptions of un-resting prayer
Pinned up in a smile
Dying because pain is not always physical
Mentally, emotionally, and spiritually exhausted
Depleted from running a race that I could only see in my mind
Overextending love just to receive a sign
That maybe I was doing something right
And I could trust the power inside
Fear has been consuming
Worried that my mistakes would keep track of my life
Not aware that the only danger was not being able to survive
This numbness
Although I was in danger
Of losing my sanity

I still write
Because if I didn't no one would know
That I was on the backside of suffering
In survival mode
          healing of things still untold
But now I am ALIVE

Now

looking back
I have defeated the very things that devoured me,
Once a upon a time

To my daughters

There is nothing more that I want to give you
Then a love that is safe
And guides you into every part of your power,
To my daughters

Love is the new money

Give me a love that is intentional and conscious
Conscious with intention
That's the new money

Fly

Fly like an eagle into the beginning
Of your new destiny
Everything is behind you

God

If had to tell you about God
I would say that God is Divine
God is a Provider
God is a Healer
God is Teacher
And these things I know

Running From Myself

I had to figure out everything about everyone
Not knowing I was running from myself
To find myself full circle

Who Am I?

I am a prayer
Who sees and hears
For an upcoming time
Intuitively prophetic
Spiritually gifted
Healer and
Creative divinely aligned

Because I Promised

Because I promised myself
To give myself more
To do more
To be more
To love more
To forgive more
To see more
To find more, in me
More than I find in others
Because I promised myself
To give myself more,
More of me
To live more
To laugh more
to spend more time with me, in me
To grow more
To learn more
To become more
More of ME

Deadlines

We are always trying to reach the destination
As if we had a deadline
WHY?
 Why is it always a race to get somewhere
When the finish line only means we have no more to receive
Or to give

Spiritually

Peace to me is a home
That is clean both
Physically and spiritually

Divine Alignment

All things intentional
Serve a plan that is beyond what we can ever witness
Because intention is beyond what we can see with our mind
It's the manifestation of all things DIVINELY revealed
And that we dream about often
Creating the ALIGNMENT of all those things coming true

CPSIA information can be obtained
at www.ICGtesting.com
Printed in the USA
BVHW060748211122
652420BV00016B/358

9 781387 496594